Silent M.a.g.i.c. and Other Remedies

Silent M.a.g.i.c. and Other Remedies

-a journey of transformation,
a spiritual journey

Kim O'Kelley-Leigh

Cover Artwork: Water Color by R.F. Leigh
The Library of Congress catalog number:
1-256669161
Copyright 2009 by Kim O'Kelley-Leigh
First Edition
ISBN 978-0-557-17890-2

This Book is Dedicated

To Randal, my beloved husband, for giving me
the space to become the best person I can be.
To Khyla, for being the greatest daughter
a mother could ever have.
To my mother Margaret, for loving me
even when I was unlovable.
To my father Pat, for your laugh
I can still hear.
To my sister Katie, for being willing to
fight for me.
To my sister Kathleen, for having so much
faith in me.
To Catherine and To Suzanne, for helping me
get this book out of my head and
onto the page.
And for your unceasing encouragement,
spelling and grammar advice.
And to all of you already practicing
Silent M.a.g.i.c., thank you
for all your love and support.

Contents

To the Reader 1

How you View your Life 3

What Happened to Me 7

Getting off the Roller Coaster 11

Cultivating a Spiritual Garden 18

Why Meditate if you have a Punishing God? 19

What If? 21

Your Relationship with God 22

An Infinite Source 26

Why Meditation is Beneficial in our Lives 27

The School of Life 30

Things aren't Always what they Seem 31

A Loving Relationship with Yourself 33

"In the Moment of Consciousness Change can Occur" 36

A Quilting Exercise 39

Gratitude 42

Lasting Happiness 46

The Hat	48
Our Relationship with Others	51
We Get what We Want	52
Letting go	55
The Ripple Effect	58
Turning Poison into Medicine	60
Conscious Choices	66
Forgiveness	68
Faith or Fear	73
A Wake-up Call	74
Taking Our Power Back	76
Trusting My Intuition	77
Beyond the Obvious	80
Great out of the Gate	82
Soul Evolution	84
My Journey with Paramahansa Yogananda	85
A Meditation in 5 Parts	89
A Visualization	92
Forever Grateful	94

To the Reader

The format of this book is unorthodox. It wasn't written in a linear fashion, nor does it have any chapters. It is comprised of probing questions, spiritual insights, practical knowledge, different fonts, and even a page upside down. But this is deliberate. It is a book designed to inspire through stories, life lessons and moments. It is about our ability to be conscious in each of these moments and to recognize that we have the power to change and live our greatest life.

This book asks you to examine your relationship with God, yourself, and with others. But it is not about religion or dogma. It is much more about cultivating your own spirituality. Silent M.a.g.i.c. gives specific tools to improve the quality of your life, and it does this in a way that anyone can understand. This book can be referred to time and time again, like a handbook, reminding us of who we truly are and of what we are capable.

"Silent M.a.g.i.c. and Other Remedies" is for everyone looking to attain true freedom, lasting happiness and inner peace. This book is from one human being to another, as we navigate through this maze we call life.

How you View your Life

The way we view life makes all the difference in the playing out of our life. We have little or no control over our outer environment, but we do have control over our inner environment, our frame of mind, and our perception of the world in which we live.

When you wake up in the morning do you find yourself thinking about what you can't have and what you can't do? Do you drag your feet throughout the day going from one drama to another? Is your attention on all the reasons you can't accomplish your goals and dreams? Do you feel wronged by others and make them wrong as well? Do you complain about everyone and everything around you? Do you hear yourself saying things like, "If they could just understand what I'm going through," "If they could just do what I say, see what I see, everything would be fine." Do you feel alone and disconnected? Are you angry, resentful, or depressed? Do you feel powerless with little hope of ever feeling good again?

There is hope!

How you View your Life

When you wake up in the morning do you look forward to each and every moment of the day? Do you sit in silence and tune into an infinite source of joy, peace, unconditional love, and wisdom that inspires you and connects you to everyone and everything? Are you a co-creator with that infinite source and therefore take responsibility for your part in each moment of your life? Are you excited to see how the day will unfold, what lessons your life is showing you? Are you grateful for all the moments of your day, and all the moments you get to express love to your family, friends, and to yourself? Is your attention on all the reasons you can accomplish your goals and dreams and be who you choose to be in each moment? Do you know that every circumstance is loving you and teaching you something about you, so that you can choose to express the greatest you that you are? Do you see opportunities in the face of obstacles? Do you have boundless energy and feel empowered in each moment? Are you living in the abundance of your life?

Just as you had to turn the book upside down to read the last page, it takes that same kind of conscious action, conscious choice, to see life from a different perspective. It takes an act of will, and a shift in our thinking.

When we view our life through eyes that are waiting for the other shoe to drop, a fear-based frame of mind, we are more easily subject to doubts, anger, frustrations, resentments, impossibilities, and lack. Thoughts of "I can't," "It's too hard," "I'm stuck," "I'm afraid," "I'm alone," consume us. Our attention is on all the things that are wrong in our lives. We are uptight, stressed out, depressed and overwhelmed. Our state of mind is negative and shut down, and we are unable to see the lessons our life is showing us. This is a victim state of consciousness and it drains us of our energy.

When we view our life through eyes that see possibilities and opportunities in each moment to grow spiritually, a faith and trust-based frame of mind, we are willing and open, joyous and content. We are able to see the beauty and love in ourselves and in all others. We are able to look at whatever needs to be changed in ourselves with a loving microscope and we make those changes with enthusiasm and gratitude. And as we change, we effect change in the people around us and in our circumstances. We are awake and ready for whatever twists and turns might be along the way. We have a calm, and stillness within, yet have infinite energy. We are able to comprehend what life is showing and teaching us, and we are getting the lessons.

The question to ask yourself is: "How can I change my fear-based frame of mind to a faith and trust-based frame of mind?" Building a daily relationship with an infinite source, a vibration, energy and intelligence, made up of joy, peace, unconditional love, and intuitional wisdom is one of the tools you can use to transform the way you view your life. The next question is "How do I do that, and what are these other tools?" This is what will be addressed in this book and so much more.

"Silent M.a.g.i.c. and Other Remedies" invites you on a journey of self-love, self-discovery, and conscious choices. This is a transformative journey, a spiritual journey, to uncover and express who you truly are.

What Happened to Me

We all experience some degree of pain in our lives, whether we bring it on ourselves or it comes from an outside source. One thing is for sure, pain can be a great motivator. A choice born out of pain is where my spiritual journey and transformation began.

I was at death's door. Drugs and alcohol had taken over my life. My actions, my thoughts, my every waking moment had everything to do with getting high, and only that. I was run by my addiction. I was consumed with fear, self-pity, desperation, anger, and resentment. The guilt, the shame, and the remorse, all came later. I was in so much mental agony, so much pain. For the last year I had been going in and out of Cocaine and Alcoholics Anonymous meetings. I would put together a few months here and there, but I wasn't able to stay clean and sober for any length of time.

I knew I wouldn't make it if I didn't get into a hospital. I found one with a two-week detox and 30-day drug program. I had to call for two weeks every morning at 7:30 am to reserve a bed space. This was the hospital's way of making sure you were serious. How I managed to do this while I was still using drugs was a miracle in itself; but I did it. I called every morning at 7:30 am, whether I was up all night stoned out of my brains or not. I got in just in time.

I was 88 pounds of skin and bones, so sick, so tired, and so afraid. I was hanging on by a thread. The only reason I could come up with for living was to watch my niece grow up. I had no desire left for my own self. Her birth was my saving grace. She was my angel.

The nightmares those first nights were so intense and so real, as if there was no separation between waking and sleeping. Well, I had been living a nightmare, that was for sure. I had created my own living hell. I was amongst the living dead. If there was a devil, I had met, slept, and eaten with him. My view of life had become so dark and negative. There was very little of the me I remembered before the drugs and alcohol. I couldn't even look in the mirror, and when I did, I hated that girl.

I lay in that hospital bed so sick to my stomach with what I'd done to myself, my life, and my family. How did I get so lost? I had come from a wonderful family and had always felt so loved and cared for by them. So much love, but look at me now. The shame, the guilt, the remorse, was all kicking in. I was in Rancho Los

Amigos Hospital for six weeks. That was in 1983.

A couple of things happened to me while I was in there. I realized I didn't want to continue living the way I had been living. And I realized I would die if I didn't change. This was my chance, and I was determined to take it. I heard a woman speak on a panel in the hospital one night about freedom, and I wanted that. I was tired of being bound by my own chains. I can still remember the hope rekindling within me while she was speaking. I knew she was speaking the truth. I was going to make it this time. I wanted sobriety. I wanted to be clean. I wanted to be free. I wanted to live.

I continued to go to AA meetings after I left the hospital and became very active in the program. I got a sponsor, cleaned up at meetings, shared, and eventually spoke at meetings. My sponsor took me through the 12 steps. I did an inventory and made amends. At six months of sobriety I began to sponsor. Then I, too, was going out to hospitals and institutions to speak and bring hope where there was very little. Once again I was experiencing gratitude for my life.

The first several years were all about staying clean and sober one day at a time, going to meetings and helping others. I thought I was working the steps, but at four and a half years of sobriety, I found myself once again in a world of pain. This time I was in pain over a man. The drugs and alcohol were gone, but the girl who couldn't look in the mirror was still there.

I was devastated by yet another broken relationship. How could I be anything else? I was living in a huge lie, a self-created lie. I was living in the belief, the delusion, that a man could bring me happiness. I was giving the man, the career, the bank account, the anything and anyone outside of myself the responsibility for my happiness. And I was doomed. I was doomed to being happy, not happy, happy, not happy, happy, not happy, over and over again.

It took the pain of another breakup to open my eyes. True happiness, lasting happiness, was an inside job. The happiness I was experiencing was only temporary. What I really wanted was a lasting happiness that had nothing to do with anything outside of myself. I wanted joy too. Remember joy?

Getting off the Roller Coaster

Once I understood what I was doing, choosing temporary happiness, I could do something about it. I had to take responsibility for my own happiness. I had been living on an emotional roller coaster, and I wanted off. I had been completely motivated by outside circumstances. How was I going to become inwardly motivated? How was I going to achieve this inward happiness that had nothing to do with the people in or not in my life, the job I may or may not have? How was I to find this lasting happiness that was unconditioned by my circumstances? I needed to go inside of myself.

Meditation was part of the 11th step in AA. I thought I was working the steps, but I hadn't been meditating. I knew this was what I needed to do. I needed to learn to meditate. It was time, and the pain I was in was overwhelming. I went to a party one afternoon, and was introduced to these two very interesting and spiritual men. After talking with them for some time, I asked them about meditation. They said I needed a mantra, which was a spiritual thought I could repeat in my mind, to bring my thoughts to just one thought. With their help I chose "I am the active expression of unconditional love at all times." I was to sit silently with my eyes closed and say that mantra for a few minutes. Then, for the remaining time, experience the stillness. At the end of the meditation I would speak from my heart whatever was on my mind.

I began with a realistic goal of five minutes a day, not being able to sit still for any longer. I knew that meditating today didn't take care of me tomorrow, so I meditated every day no matter what. After a month I went to seven minutes a day. I had an egg timer set for the minutes to help me. I continued to increase my minutes until I was doing twenty minutes every morning.

As the days, weeks, and months went by, I became thirsty for spiritual knowledge, devouring many a book. *Be Here Now* by Ram Das, *The Road Less Traveled* by M. Scott Peck, *Living in the Light* by Shakti Gawain, *Way of the Peaceful Warrior* by Dan Millman, *The Greatest Miracle in the World* by Og Mandino, *The Celestine Prophecy* by James Redfield, and *The Seat of the Soul* by Gary Zukav, to name a few.

The more spiritual knowledge I gathered, and as my time in meditation increased, I experimented with different techniques. I worked with observing my breath, with the seven chakras, and with different visualizations. I continued to expand my awareness, hone my understanding, deepen my gratitude, and cultivate my daily practice. I was being guided by my own meditation.

The reasons I began to meditate started with what I was going to get, and what meditation could do for me. I wanted to become inwardly motivated. I wanted to own my own happiness. I wanted to calm my restless mind. I wanted. I wanted. I see now that my consciousness, my attention, was focused on what I wanted and what I was going to get. This was true not only in meditation, but in every relationship I was in. All about me I was. Just like a child, totally self-centered. Yet I was thirty-one years old now, not eight. As I continued to meditate daily, the reasons that brought me to meditation began to change. As if by silent magic, I was being transformed.

***Meditation is the bridge that transforms
the "me" consciousness
to the "we" consciousness
to the "you" consciousness.***

Early on in my meditation process, I realized that I needed to look at and question the relationship I had with God. I had never really thought about it before. I had been raised Methodist, but what did that really mean, and what did that religion have to do with my relationship with God? And while I was digging and probing, what was God to me anyway? Was God a little old man up in heaven running my life, rewarding me when I was good and punishing me when I was bad? And what was heaven? And was God a person? No, that didn't feel right. What about love, God as love? Not a selfish, human love, but unconditional love. That felt more like it, and what about God as joy and wisdom and peace? And what if I expressed these qualities? Wasn't that expressing God in my life? If I began to cultivate a relationship in meditation with these qualities that I called "God," wasn't that building a relationship with a God of my own understanding? Yes, it was.

I also began to look more honestly at myself. The who I thought I was and the who I had become were two different people. I had always considered myself to be a positive and happy person. Maybe I was at one time, or when I was a child, but that girl was nowhere in sight. She'd been buried under my life's experiences. I realized I didn't like myself. My actions had brought me there, and my thinking was not only negative about myself, but negative about the world and everyone else. I had heard someone say that if you wanted to change a tape you had to re-record over it. My negative thoughts were just that, a tape playing over and over again. Unless I re-recorded over them, they were not going to change.

I had gone to the Bodhi Tree, a metaphysical bookstore in Los Angeles, and had been drawn to two books. *You Can Heal Your Life* by Louise Hay and *Metaphysical Meditations* by Paramahansa Yogananda. Among many amazing ideas, Hay introduced me to mirror work, which was saying positive affirmations into the mirror. At the end of each of her chapters she had affirmations that always began with "In the infinity of life where I am, all is perfect, whole, and complete." She continued on with positive thoughts of acceptance, trusting the universe, letting go of the past and more. I read her words and felt they were true, but I didn't believe half of them.

Nevertheless, after I meditated in the morning, I began to read her affirmations at the end of each chapter into the mirror. I also chose to read into the mirror several passages from Yogananda's book. His words were so profound, they brought tears to my eyes and they touched my soul. Here are a few examples: "I am beholding through the eyes of all. I am working through all hands, I am walking through all feet. The brown, white, olive, yellow, red, and black bodies are all mine." "I am the wind of wisdom that dries the sighs and sorrows of all humanity. I am the silent joy of life moving through all beings."

Intuitively I knew that saying these words into the mirror on a daily basis would change my life, not to mention my negative thinking. So each morning after I meditated, I showed up to the mirror for 20 to 30 minutes a day. I did this mirror work for six months, and by the end of the six months my thinking and my view of life was changing. All the affirmations were becoming true to me. Little by little the negative thoughts were being recorded over. I was changing my habitual tape and giving myself a positive brainwashing.

Another very profound thing happened. I began to see a beauty inside of myself that surpassed all physical beauty. When I first started looking in the mirror all I could see was my physical self, the lines, the blemishes, the age on my face, and with that, came all negative thoughts having to do with my imperfections. I was seeing only the surface, the physical, and the personality me. As the days went by continuing the affirmations, I began to see in my reflection the infinity of my soul: all beauty, all wisdom, all joy, and all light inside of me. I was experiencing a connection to all life, a we inside of me. And I knew it was for all of us willing to make the effort.

I also began changing my actions and my habitual behavior. So many of the habits I had built had been built unconsciously. I never set out consciously to be a self-centered person, a fearful, impatient, or judgmental person. So with the help of a loving microscope, I began to take one action, one thought at a time, and weave a new me.

With the daily practice of meditation, affirmations, gratitude, inward motivation, and conscious choices, I was transforming my life one moment at a time. The pain I experienced, ended up being a springboard to an amazing spiritual journey.

*Being awake and conscious
gives us the ability to dig ourselves,
to hear and know our thoughts,
and to see our actions
and reactions.*

Cultivating a Spiritual Garden

Our flowers are patience, kindness, generosity, unconditional love, trust, faith, peace, serenity, wisdom, abundance, joy and bliss. Every flower needs sunshine, water, pruning, care and tending. ***Meditation***, calming the restless mind and tuning in and connecting to an infinite source, is the sunshine. ***Affirmations***, replacing negative thoughts with positive ones, is the watering. ***Gratitude***, being thankful for what we have and for what we don't have, is the pruning. ***Inward Motivation***, taking responsibility for our own happiness, is the care. And ***Conscious Choices***, changing habitual negative actions and re-actions in the moment, is the tending. The daily practice of these is our spiritual well being.

Weeds, on the other hand, grow and spread and take over our garden at a very fast rate. The weeds are fear, doubt, anger, envy, jealousy, greed, lack, self-pity, selfishness, impatience, restless discontent, anxiety, indecision, ignorance and indifference. The daily practice of these creates dis-ease. Are we taking care of our flowers and uprooting the weeds?

What is growing in your garden?

Why Meditate if you have a Punishing God?

When you close your eyes and sit very still and quiet, what do you feel? Do you feel alone, or do you feel a connection to all life? Are you uneasy, discontented, and fearful, or are you peaceful, joyous, and calm? Do you feel scrutinized and punished, or loved and cared for? Do you see the possibilities in your life, or are they only for others, and not for you? If you feel alone, uneasy, fearful, punished and scrutinized, you may need an overhaul in your belief system where God is concerned.

I was working with a girl several years ago, teaching her to meditate. She kept coming up with reasons why she couldn't meditate. She couldn't sit still. She couldn't stop her thoughts. She didn't have the time. And when she did try to meditate, she felt uneasy. I decided to ask her questions about her childhood and what she thought about God.

She told me she was raised in a specific religion and had grown up very angry with God. *He* had not answered her prayers when she had really needed *him* to answer. She was convinced that *he* punished her when she was bad and rewarded her when she was good, whatever that meant, because she knew she wasn't good, not anymore. *He* abandoned her. She abandoned *him*. In her mind, God was not only something outside of herself, but *he* wasn't there for her at all. She didn't want any part of meditating, not with this God that was going to send her to hell.

No wonder she was having trouble. She needed to find a way to release that old idea of God and replace it with unconditional love, or nature, or something other than what she had. She needed to find and develop a God of her own understanding, so she could sit in the stillness and silence. Until she made the effort to address her anger, shame and resentment, and redefine her concept of God, there was no way she would choose to meditate. These were the obstacles keeping her from building and maintaining a daily meditation practice.

Let's face it, would you consciously choose to develop a daily relationship in meditation with one who punished you, who abandoned you, and was always disappointed by you? No, you wouldn't. No one would, and no one does. What about meditating with an infinite source of unconditional love?

What If?

What if we were awake and fully conscious in each moment? How would that change our lives? What if all the answers to all our questions were inside of us, and all we had to do was listen and remember? What if every opportunity was designed to evolve us spiritually? What if God were a vibration, energy and intelligence, an infinite source made up of unconditional love, joy, peace, wisdom, and bliss? What if God were an infinite source accessible to us all, ever new, ever flowing in and around us? What if we were co-creators with this infinite source and intelligence? What would our part be? What if every circumstance, every relationship with others, was the means to express this infinite source? What if every outward situation and every circumstance was our teacher, showing us just what we needed to learn to move us further along the spiritual path?

Your Relationship with God

You were either raised in a specific religion, i.e. Catholic, Protestant, Moslem, Jewish, Christian, Hindu, Buddhist, etc, or raised in a non-religious family, or raised agnostic or atheist. No matter what category you fall into, you have some relationship with God, whether you call it God, or Nature, the Universe, Great Spirit, Krishna, Buddha, Jesus, Divine Mother, Allah, or any other name or meaning, or none at all. It seems to me that this relationship affects everything that we think and do.

For some of you, religion works. You are comforted and made better by the teachings you're following. You have a great sense of peace, and respect for other people and for other religions. You have a strong sense of faith that sees you through the challenging times in your life.

For other people, their particular religious beliefs have given them a justifiable reason to kill others. They use religion to justify their prejudices, and disdain for others not like them. They use religious scriptures to bring out the differences between religions. They find fault in others' beliefs with a determination to prove why their way is the right way, and why everyone needs to believe the way they believe.

For some, God has become a buzzword that triggers all sorts of negative emotions, turning them off religion altogether. Maybe a religious person harmed them, or maybe they just became disillusioned.

What if you were raised with the idea there is no God? God is for the poor and needy. Religion is for the weak. You may have less guilt, less fear of the end of the world, although you may have a sense of separation, an emptiness inside.

Many of you have been handed down a religion, only to find that you have no real connection, or real relationship to that religion. You may go through the motions of going to church or temple; you may pray and even turn to God for help, but generally you have little faith in this hand-me-down religion.

Does this sound familiar?

Do you find yourself bargaining with God, telling *him* what *he* should do to make your life work? Do you have a God that is out there somewhere, a God that you frequently criticize and complain to, a God that can punish you for your sins and your wrongs, a God that can give you your needs if you deserve it? Do you have a God that you fear, and kind of want to know, but generally don't think in terms of hanging out with this *guy*, this *he*, this God, unless *he* is giving you what you want. This is a condition-based relationship. You find fault in *him*. *He* finds fault in you. We all say "*He*" out of conditioning. This idea of "*He*" needs to be investigated.

We live in a world of finding fault in ourselves, in others, and in God. If God's part is to listen when *he* wants to, help you when *he* deems you worthy, promise you heaven if you do what *he* says and hell if you don't, your part is what? Sit back and wait to be told what to do? Try to live by *his* rules? Pray to this *guy*, this God, to annihilate your neighbor in his name?

This is an old Dark Ages idea of God. Talk about feeling powerless. How about angry, resentful, unmotivated, and depressed? No wonder half the world is on some kind of legal or illegal medication. Have you noticed how many religious wars have taken place in the world and are still taking place? With an idea of God such as this, how could anyone sit on a daily basis and meditate?

The thing is, you can be any religion, or no religion at all, and meditate. You can close your eyes and sit with any great soul in meditation: Jesus, Buddha, Krishna, Mohammed, all the great saints and sages of all religions if you choose to, or not.

Look at and re-evaluate your relationship, if any, with God. Do some writing about what God is to you. Write about the religion you were raised in or not raised in. Write about what is working and not working. And if the word "God" sends you into a tailspin, use a different word. Look at any emotional issues surrounding God. Journaling is a great tool. Be willing to smash any old ideas regarding God. Be willing to create new ones. Be willing to develop an understanding of God that can grow inside of you and take you past the believing in God, to a direct personal experience of God. Sitting in meditation is where we can cultivate, build, and experience this relationship.

Discover what your stumbling blocks, if any, to meditation are, and turn them into building blocks. They are your teachers. This is how we transform obstacles into opportunities.

An Infinite Source

There is an infinite source, an energy, a vibration, that radiates all beauty, all joy, all wisdom, all peace, all abundance, and all power. This source of unconditional love is ever flowing, ever expressing itself through all life and all beings. We are connected by this source, and by tuning into this source, we reawaken the knowledge inside ourselves that we are all the same. We are soul, expressing a myriad of personalities, yet we're not these personalities. These personalities are the illusions that separate us, and yet there is no separation. We are all the same as we connect and receive this source. We internalize our oneness, and then actualize this oneness through each choice we make in each moment we have. We are this unending flow of joy, peace, wisdom, beauty, unconditional love, compassion, bliss, serenity, patience, and gratitude, ever expressing itself continually.

This infinite source is what God is to me. Being one with God is expressing these energies in each moment of my life. Meditation is how I connect and tune my consciousness to this source.

Why Meditation is Beneficial in our Lives

When we begin to meditate, mostly what draws us to meditation is what it will do for us, and how it will improve our lives. Along the way is where the transformation of our lives occurs. We transform in many ways. We can go from a consciousness of what we can get, to a consciousness of what we can give. We can go from being outwardly motivated to being inwardly motivated. Our view of life can change from being screwed, cursed, separate, and alone, to being a part of an infinite source of joy, unconditional love, wisdom, and peace. The reasons we meditate change in time. The questions we ask along the way change as well.

The nature of the mind is restless, moving in and out of thoughts of the past, and thoughts of the future. Thoughts of the past can bring in resentments and regrets. Thoughts of the future can contain fears. Meditation is where we can calm our restless mind and experience the present moment. The present moment is where all conscious choices are alive. The present moment is where we can cultivate and build a relationship with an infinite source made up of unconditional love, joy, peace, and intuitional wisdom. Meditation is where we can develop and strengthen our intuition, our sixth sense. And a developed intuition is always true. Each time we meditate and turn our attention and energy inward, we expand our awareness of this infinite source, ourselves and of others, and deepen our levels of consciousness. We sit in the silence of meditation, and remember who we truly are. We just need to push past the surface of our restless mind to realize we are not the body, or the mind. We are soul. We are light. We are ever-new joy and bliss. This is our true nature. We are spiritual beings continuously connected. It is our restlessness that keeps this truth hidden, and when we contact and experience our true nature all-else pales in comparison.

Every morning when I wake up, and every evening, I make a conscious choice to meditate and tune into and connect with a presence, an energy, a vibration, an infinite source that radiates all joy, peace, unconditional love, and wisdom. I sit in each present moment experiencing the now. I sit and experience a deep gratitude for all that I have, and all that I don't have. This is the gift I give myself. I give myself this time to align with these energies, so throughout my day I am more easily able to express these energies in my daily life.

What kinds of energy are you expressing? What kinds of thoughts are you thinking? What is your attention on?

The ocean is in the wave and the wave is in the ocean. Liken your personality to the wave, individualized and limited. Then liken your soul to the ocean, expansive and unlimited. Now think, feel, and imagine the amount of joy, peace, wisdom, and unconditional love a wave contains. Then think, feel and imagine the amount of joy, peace, wisdom, and unconditional love the ocean contains.
The wave is in the ocean and the ocean is in the wave. What is your attention on, the ocean or the wave?

The School of Life

What if the earth plane was a school to learn our life lessons? What would those life lessons be? What if everything that happens in our life is exactly what we need to grow spiritually? What if every moment we experience is an opportunity for us to deepen our abilities to become more selfless, more patient, more compassionate, more joyous, more courageous, more unconditionally loving, and more trusting?

What if we were co-creators with an infinite source of joy, peace, unconditional love, and wisdom, and together we were teaching ourselves how to get back home? What if home was being one with this infinite source?

I am asking you to look at your life from possibly a different perspective. I am asking you to consider that your life is giving you an opportunity to deepen your levels of consciousness, expand your awareness, and to express your highest and greatest self.

How can we become aware of our life lessons? How can we look past the surface of our daily circumstances and relationships to find a deeper meaning?

Things aren't Always what they Seem

I went to a parent education meeting one evening at my daughter's elementary school to learn about testing, I thought. When I got there I found out the talk was about a very specific test called the ISEE. This is a test only given to children applying for private middle or high school. I heard myself saying, "I don't know what I'm doing here then."

In my mind, within moments, a slew of negative thoughts followed about financial lack now, and the financial lack I was projecting into the future. I had so many thoughts about what other people might be thinking about me, and why was I there, and didn't I realize I wasn't going to get to send my daughter to another private school? If I were lucky, she would get another year at this private school, and on and on.

This all happened within seconds, mind you. Then suddenly I realized I wasn't there to learn about the test at all. I was there to learn about my own "lack" consciousness. I recognized a thought pattern, a habitual mode of thinking that said, "Now, and in the future, we don't have enough money. We don't have enough money for another private school or anything else. We don't have enough." I was there to learn a life lesson.

Thoughts create, and my thoughts were creating my own financial lack based on a habitual mode of thinking. I was being shown that without uprooting these thoughts of lack, these habitual grooves in my record, I was condemning myself to creating the same reality over and over again.

Just wanting financial freedom wasn't enough. I needed to change my thinking and my actions in order to create a new reality. I needed to look honestly at my situation in order to ascertain the best course of action to take in attaining financial freedom. I also needed to replace my thoughts of lack with thoughts of abundance every time I became aware of them. This was the reason I was at that parent meeting.

We are so conditioned to look for answers and knowledge on the outside. What about the answers and knowledge we have on the inside?

Discovering our life lessons is part of the spiritual journey.
It takes time, but it can be done.

A Loving Relationship with Yourself

Being on a spiritual path is a journey, not a destination. It is made up of moments, one moment at a time. Along the way, as we begin to wake up, we can place our attention on our own habitual behavior and thinking. We have many chances for do-overs.

How would you describe the relationship you have with yourself? Are you loving, kind and gentle, or do you make yourself wrong and beat yourself up? "You are so adorable." Is that a phrase you hear yourself saying to yourself? Or is it more like, "You idiot"? When you look into the mirror what do you see? Can you say "I love you," and mean it? What thoughts about yourself come back to you? Do you only see the flaws in your face, your age lines, your crooked nose, your blemishes, or can you see past your physical self and recognize your inner beauty?

Your relationship with yourself has just as much to do with how you think about yourself as with the behavior you express. Are you aware of how you think about yourself? What are your habitual thought patterns? Are you in a no-hope thinking wheel? Do you have a victim consciousness mentality? Have you ever even slowed down long enough to find out?

How we think affects how we act. How we act affects how we think. What comes first? This is up for debate. Some people say you can't think yourself into right action, you can only act yourself into right thinking. I know you can do both. Change your actions, and as a result of that change, your thinking changes. Change your thinking, and it results in changing your actions. Some people understand how to change an action, but how do we change our thinking? As I said earlier, if you want to get rid of what's on a cassette tape you have to re-record over it. Likewise, we have to re-record over our negative thoughts with positive ones. We can give ourselves a positive brainwashing.

Affirmations are great tools in changing our thinking. The mirror work I did at the beginning of my journey was life changing. So much so, that over the years I have worked with men and women one-on-one, and in a classroom situation, teaching them how to use affirmations into the mirror as a tool to build a loving connection with themselves. You can create your own affirmations by listening to your own thoughts. For example: "I'm all alone." Change that to "I am connected to everyone and everything." You can also use the books I used or go on the Internet and find hundreds of sites with positive affirmations. All you need is to be willing, and the help you need, will come your way.

Along with saying the affirmations into the mirror, we want to change any negative thinking we become aware of in the moment. I was given this thought in meditation one morning. *"In the moment of consciousness change can occur,"* "can" being the operative word. I have used this thought in so many situations to help me create a change right in the moment.

The way we think can be self-pitying, negative, fault-finding, and closed, or it can be positive, solution-oriented, questioning, and open. If we can become aware and conscious of our thinking and of our actions in the moment, we can then choose to change our habitual negative thoughts and actions by creating new and positive ones.

We have many chances for do-overs.

"In the Moment of Consciousness Change can Occur"

I was with a friend the other day, and she began telling me about this man she was going to have a date with on Friday night. She was really excited that a man she was attracted to was also attracted to her. Then she said, "Once he finds out my full name he's going to Google me and see that I'm fifty years old and not want to go out with me anymore." She continued to tell me how this always happens to her and maybe she needs to change her name so no one can look her up on the Internet.

I looked at her and said, "Why are you bringing the past into this present moment? In the moment of consciousness change can occur. Right now you can change that thought and affirm you are open and willing for a new experience. If you re-record over that thought you will stop creating more of the same."

She was totally closed to hearing that she had anything to do with this continuing to happen to her. As far as she was concerned, this was the way men were, and she had no part in it. She could not see how this thought, created from a reaction to a time in her past, was coloring her present. After I realized she was closed to what I was saying, I let it go.

All of a sudden she started screaming that the bottle of water in her purse was leaking all over her cell phone. She grabbed the bottle and threw it on the ground. I picked it up and said, "Look, the cap is loose." She couldn't hear me. She was too caught up in freaking out and blaming the bottle of water for ruining her phone.

Blaming the bottle was like blaming the men. This was the perfect circumstance to illustrate what I had been talking about. I was hoping that she would put these moments together, see her part in each of them, and have a realization of what I'd been saying. If she continues to think that men don't want her when they find out that she is fifty, this is exactly what she will attract: men who don't want her because of her age. And if it's the bottle's fault, she will ruin many a cell phone. This is a victim state of consciousness: "It's their fault that I'm the way I am or that I am in the situation I'm in." I don't think she ever saw what I saw. Maybe the scenarios were just for me to affirm what I knew.

Seeing our part is the best way to avoid creating more of the same. Our thoughts and our actions create, and we need to learn to take responsibility for what they are creating. Why do we find it so difficult to see our part in life?

Maybe it's because blaming others is the best way to avoid looking honestly at ourselves. Maybe it's because when it is our part, the only thing we know how to do is call ourselves stupid, or failures, and beat ourselves up for the mistakes. Maybe we need to learn how to be more loving to ourselves when we make mistakes. Mistakes are a part of life, and there is no getting around them, but we can choose to learn from them.

Introspection can be a damaging tool if we pick up a baseball bat, metaphorically speaking, and beat ourselves up with it. But it can be a wonderful tool if we look at ourselves with a loving microscope.

To enter the door of change, we must first become aware of what needs to be changed.

A Quilting Exercise

I first began to notice my impatience while I was driving. When I was in a hurry, everyone on the road was slow. One day I saw myself being so impatient and anxious while driving, beeping the horn at cars, talking to people even though they couldn't hear me. "Go, go, go! What are you doing?" "What's wrong with you people?" I was miserable, angry, uptight, anxious, and clearly impatient. Why did I want to continue to be this way? I didn't. *In the moment of consciousness change can occur*. This was the thought that was going to help me change. The next time I noticed myself being impatient was the next time I had the chance to be that much closer to being a patient person.

I was in my car again, and here was my chance: there was a slowpoke in front of me. Instead of beeping my horn and acting out of my impatience, I said to myself, "I can manifest patience right now. In this moment of consciousness, instead of actualizing my habit of impatience, I can choose to act opposite of my habit." Habit, that's important to remember. I didn't beep my horn or talk to the person who couldn't hear me anyway. I also didn't live in my justification of why the other person was wrong. I sat patiently. By manifesting patience, I felt calm and peaceful, not anxious and angry. Anxiousness and anger came with the habit of impatience. Calmness and contentment came with the patient behavior.

I began to realize that if I wanted to be a patient person, I had to begin to sew together moments like this one over and over again. Through breaking the habit of impatience, moment-to-moment, step-by-step, I was becoming a patient person. Once I achieved a character change in this area, I realized that I was capable of change in any area.

Like a quilt or tapestry, I began to weave together moments of my life to become the kind of person I wanted to be. I didn't set out to be an impatient person. I had unconsciously built a habit of impatient moments; and then one day I woke up to an impatient person. Self-centeredness was another area I wanted to change in myself. I had to notice when I was being self-centered and in that moment make a choice to be selfless. Instead of having a conversation with another person revolving around me, I began to ask about the other person. I began to listen, not just talk.

Anything in yourself that you want to change, you can. As we become conscious of our thoughts and actions, we can then determine which thoughts and actions need to be transformed. We can begin to make conscious choices in the moment, as opposed to reacting habitually. We need to see in our own behavior where we are on autopilot. Autopilot means where we are asleep, and where we are repeating habits created unconsciously. We all have them.

Fortunately, we all have choices too. We just don't know how to make these conscious choices and be a co-creator in life, as opposed to a victim of life's circumstances. Isn't making conscious choices in the moment preferable to being on autopilot?

We are like a beautiful quilt.
We can sew this quilt to be whatever
we choose, square by square.
We can shape our lives,
moment by moment,
one square at a time.

Gratitude

There is always something to be grateful for, if we look for it. There is always something to be ungrateful for, if we look for that. With a past like mine, how can I be anything but grateful for each moment of my life today? My past has brought me to gratitude, but this is not the case for everyone.

There are many people who have had a past like mine, or a past riddled with pain, that has brought them to anger, resentment, and bitterness. They stay in their reactions never getting to the place of being grateful. They are unable or unwilling to find anything to be grateful for. All they see and feel is injustice. They live in a world of what could have been or should be.

Gratitude is a choice and an action. It is an expression found in that moment just after reaction. Moving from reaction to gratitude can be a short or long road, but this road is worth taking to get to our final destination. Stopping short can only keep our hearts embroiled in pain. Being grateful for what we have and for what we don't have takes practice. The more we express gratitude, the more we feel grateful.

Gratitude as a state of mind can be found in the way we view our life. If we know that everything is in perfect order, we are more easily able to express gratitude in any given situation. We can always travel from our first reaction to gratitude because we know that all things are happening for a reason, and we trust in this perfect order of life. Meditation grows our ability to live in gratitude.

How can we express being grateful in each moment when some moments fill us with anything but gratitude? When something or someone is taken from us, our initial reaction is usually not one of gratitude. But that doesn't mean we can't decide to live in gratitude after that initial reaction.

My father had gone into the hospital for surgery. I called him after the surgery to see how he was doing, and he said it had been successful. Inside I heard he was not going to live, but I brushed that thought out of my mind. That was a Friday night. Saturday night we spoke again and what I remember about that conversation was we laughed a lot, and he said he loved me. This was a common occurrence between us, laughter and exchanging 'I love you's." Early Sunday morning he had a stroke. When I spoke with him that morning he was unable to really talk. The stroke had affected his speech. His words were never understandable again. My dad died three days later of that stroke at the age of 68.

My father was a man loved by his family and friends, and he made sure we all knew he loved us. My parents were high school sweethearts. They literally grew up together. They were married just shy of 50 years, and in love for 53 years. It doesn't get better than that.

It was a shock for everyone when he died. He was so young. It was unfair. The doctors must have made a mistake. Why did this have to happen? Trying to find what went wrong didn't last very long. My mother had raised us to look for the good in life. Almost collectively we began talking about how grateful we were that Daddy got to go so quickly.

My mother and sister were at his side when he passed out of his body. They said he had a look of peace on his face. My father would have definitely not liked being in a body that didn't work. And we all knew he wouldn't have wanted to live that way. How fortunate we all were that we had such a great father, and for our mother, that she had a wonderful loving husband. We decided to stay focused on all the love we shared.

The memorial service was more of a celebration, as family and friends gathered to honor his life. This isn't to say that we didn't cry or feel a great loss, but the underlying current was gratitude for the time we got to have with him. Living in our loss would only bring unhappiness.

And he wanted us to be happy.

It has been eight years now since his passing. And even though his body is gone, he is still very much alive in spirit and in my heart. I have to pick up a phone to talk to my mom, but with my dad I can talk to him anytime. I still feel his love and hear his laughter. I continue to feel grateful for having had the time with Daddy that we did have. We all have chosen to remember him with a joyous heart.

*Being grateful for what we have,
and for what we don't have,
is a conscious choice.*

Lasting Happiness

There is an imaginary hole inside of us that we are trying to fill up to make us happy, content, and connected. We try to fill this imaginary hole with many different experiences and in many different ways. We use alcohol, drugs, food, cigarettes, relationships, work, vacations, shopping, money, people, places, and things, to try and achieve that well-being, that happiness, that contentment, connectivity, and security. The one thing they all have in common is they all come from an outside source. The problem is, our happiness from these things can only be temporary.

When we tune into an infinite source of peace, joy, unconditional love, and wisdom on a daily basis, we begin to experience an internal happiness that outshines any temporary, external experience of happiness we could ever have. The imaginary hole dissolves. Our happiness becomes rooted in the relationship and connection we have with this infinite source and ceases to have anything to do with what's going on outside of ourselves. And, most importantly, it ceases to be temporary. Maybe joy is the deeper level of happiness? Maybe joy is the constant, where happiness is the temporary? Lasting happiness, joy, has everything to do with our relationship with this infinite source, whether we call it God or not.

We are in charge and responsible for tuning in, and ultimately giving ourselves back the power over our own happiness. We have the power to experience and express unconditional love and gratitude in each moment of our lives. We have the power to feel connected to all life or not. We have the power to become inwardly motivated.

Lasting happiness is an inside job.

The Hat

The other night before I began to meditate, I took off the hat I had been wearing that day to keep my head warm. As I was meditating it began to feel as if the hat was still on my head, but I knew I had taken it off. The feeling was so real. It must still be there, but how? Then the information came flooding in on me. So many times in life we convince ourselves that something is real, and yet we come to see we were just making it real. Our thoughts convince us, and, instead of going with the truth, we buy the lie. The hat not being on my head was the symbol for these times. It reminded me how important it is to live in the truth, and to uproot our own self-created lies built on fantasy.

For instance, have you ever told yourself that you were stuck in a relationship? You really wanted to be out, but you were stuck? That is like the imaginary hat. The thought is just a thought. And we either choose to make that thought real or not real. By making the thought that you are stuck real, you are condemning yourself to a victim consciousness and a no-hope scenario. By choosing to replace the thought of "I'm stuck" to something like, "I am willing and able to change my circumstances," you begin to unravel the lie you've been making real. As you revolve that new positive thought around in your mind, "I am willing and able to change my circumstances," you begin to change your thinking. You then create energy within yourself to make the change, and, in turn, you begin to change your inner environment. This then gives you the permission and ability to make changes to your outer environment, changing on the inside first as opposed to trying to make a change on the outside first. This is one of the steps in becoming inwardly motivated.

There is no energy in the "I'm stuck" mentality. Isn't that mentality, that way of thinking, a reaction to our circumstances, and therefore keeping us outwardly motivated? Thoughts of "I'm stuck," give us no possibilities and lead us to actions of no energy and ultimately depression. Thoughts of "I am willing and able to change my circumstances," give us possibilities, and possibilities lead us to actions and the energy to create the change.

So many of our thought patterns were created with an unconscious mind, our thoughts weren't built on consciousness and truth; they were built on a self-created lie, and on reactions. We want to listen to our thoughts, to know what thoughts need to be replaced to achieve a different outcome in our lives. Keep this in mind when replacing a habitual negative thought. If we think or say "I want to be less judgmental," we create more judgmental moments. The "less" gets lost in the translation. Just as when we say "I want to be more compassionate," the "more" gets lost as well. Here are the two different statements without the adverbs "less" and "more." "I want to be judgmental." "I want to be compassionate." For this reason, we want to affirm what we want, not what we don't want.

Being awake and conscious gives us the ability to dig ourselves, to hear and to know our thoughts, and to see our actions and reactions. So when we hear ourselves think or say what we don't want, we can immediately replace it with an affirmation of what we do want. This is a chance for a do-over. There are many chances for do-overs in life, when you think about it.

> ***"We are what we repeatedly do.***
> ***Excellence, therefore,***
> ***is not an act but a habit"***
>
> *-Aristotle*

Our Relationship with Others

It seems very easy to see what other people need to do differently in any given situation. We give advice on what they need to do, what they need to learn, and how they need to go about accomplishing these things, whether it is solicited or not. When we keep our eyes and our attention on the other person and their faults, we have no time left to see our own. We lose sight of what we need to do and what our life is showing us to work on. This doesn't mean that others don't have faults or wrong behavior. It means that if we focus on others and where they are wrong, we stop focusing on our own part, and where we can improve. It's really none of our business what another person needs to change in themselves, unless they ask our opinion, or for our help.

The way we are with others begins to change the more we change. As we become inwardly motivated, we become more responsible for our own happiness, and then we begin to find new meaning in our relationships with others. They become the greatest avenues through which we can grow spiritually.

We Get what We Want

What if that statement were true? What if every relationship, every situation, every happening in our lives was what we wanted? Could you look at your life right now and say that was true?

At one point in my life, I was going from one failed relationship to the next by constantly picking the unavailable man. I was complaining to a good friend one day about my latest heartbreak and how I wanted to get married. She stopped me and said, "You don't want to get married. You want exactly what you're getting." "That is not true!" I said, and went on to complain some more.

Later that evening, I took what she had said to me into meditation. As long as I continued to take the position, "I'm not getting what I want, and it's the guy's fault for being unattainable," I was leaving myself in a powerless state, a victim state of consciousness. I wasn't changing my choices or accepting any responsibility for my own actions. All I was doing was complaining about the situation, then blaming the situation, and then repeating the same choices that were causing me pain. I was caught in a habit of choosing pain. That was the bottom line. I was on autopilot. My habit was driving me, and I was in the passenger seat.

When I looked at the real possibility that I was getting what I wanted, it woke me up. I began to see how I was continually creating, out of habit, what I didn't want. It was now time to begin to create what I did want. I needed to make some serious changes, not only in my actions but in my thinking as well. Here's what I was doing. I would have a physical, a chemical attraction to a man, sleep with him, and then go to sleep in my consciousness. I would act on that chemistry and not take the time to see if we were compatible on any other level. My whole basis was a physical and chemical attraction. I left out the mental and spiritual levels of attraction.

One morning I got this vision of a man standing a mile or so down a long straight road. On both sides of the road was a desert. This vision was a metaphor. The desert represented the unavailable guy. The man down the road represented my husband-to-be. Every time I acted on my chemical attraction, it was the same as being thrown into the desert, stripped of my choices, and destined to remain there until the desert spit me out. As soon as I stepped one foot into the desert, I was lost. I had no control. There was no controlling the desert.

My only hope was not to choose the desert in the first place, not to act on my chemical attraction. I realized that if the man down that road was to be my husband, all I had to do was walk forward. As long as I chose the desert, I was lateralizing my life. I wasn't moving forward at all. The desert would spit me back out at the same place on the road I was before I went into the desert.

Within the next few months I was presented the opportunity of the desert four more times. Only now, I was hip to the truth within myself, and I wanted no part of the desert. I released myself from the grips of choosing pain. I owned my choices, and now I walked proudly by. What do you figure happened? Yes, I walked straight to the man that would become my husband. Only this time I was attracted to him on all levels: spiritually, mentally, physically and chemically. We were married one year later and still are to this day.

Are you getting what you want?

Letting go

From the moment of conception to our last breath, we are in a process of letting go. In each stage of our lives, there are thousands of times we are called on to let go. We have to let go of the womb, the breast or bottle, crawling to walk, babyhood to childhood, teenage years to young adulthood, and adulthood to old age. And what about letting go of unconsciously built habits, or letting go of the past? How about letting go of the world as we go deeper into meditation? How do we know when and what to let go of? How do we prepare ourselves to let go, even when we don't want to? Isn't death of our body the last ultimate letting go?

When I first met my husband, he gave me his phone number and asked me to call him if I was interested in going out. I started to shake. There was something different about him. I knew if I went out with him, it would change my life. After that night, I meditated for twelve days before I got the sense that it would be all right to call. By this time in my life I had been meditating for seven years, and I didn't make any major decisions without taking them into meditation. I also had an intuition that night that he didn't want to have children. I had always wanted children. I had even written a lullaby for my future child. After the first couple of dates, besides having a wonderful connection, my intuition was confirmed. He, in fact, wasn't interested in having kids. Was this going to present a problem for us?

Luckily, I had been hired to do a play in Colorado for a month, so that gave me some time away to think about him and the great connection we had. We spoke only once while I was there, and when I got back we decided to continue to get to know each other. The months began to fly by and we were getting closer. I soon realized I had to consider marrying a man that didn't want children. I would either have to let go of my lifelong desire to have children, or walk away from this amazing man. I took this new dilemma into meditation.

I saw an equation in my mind that said having children = happiness. How did this slip by? I already knew that happiness was an inside job. Here I was giving a child the care of my happiness. I needed to let go of this equation and smashing it was my answer. How many other false equations did I have, and how many more of them needed to be eliminated? I made a mental note: be on the lookout for false equations. Were these circumstances to teach me about having equations in my head? Or were they teaching me about letting go? It seems I had a new lesson to learn, and an old one to revisit and deepen.

I made a conscious choice to apply these lessons and let go of my desire to have children. We were married. If I were meant to be a mother, that day would come to pass, not by fulfilling an equation in my head, or holding on to a desire, or by trying to change his mind. Six months into our marriage, he came to me and said he wanted to have a child. It felt like a miracle. He had changed his own mind without any prodding from me. I had let go and trusted the lessons in front of me, and ended up getting exactly what I wanted... a beautiful daughter.

Letting go is a choice.
It takes moving through resistance
and a fear of the unknown.
It takes another choice of willingness
to move past the unknown.

The Ripple Effect

When we throw a pebble into a lake, there is a ripple that begins to grow out of the very first contact to the water. Our thoughts and actions have this same ripple effect. We all have the ability to uplift everyone we come in contact with, if we choose to, by every thought and action we take. Think about this scenario:

You are driving in your car (there is something about life lessons and cars) and someone comes out of nowhere and cuts you off. Do you lean on the horn and begin yelling obscenities giving him or her the finger? Or do you give the person a knowing look that says, "I've done that too," and make no judgment? The first way is reactionary, full of anger and resentment. The second way is a choice, finding similarities in the behavior and expressing compassion for the mistake.

Think about what the other person takes away after each encounter. Most likely after the first one, he'll take that negative energy you've given him and store it up until he hands it out to the next person who cuts him off. The same holds true for the second encounter, only it's positive energy he will store up and hand out.

If we look at our thoughts and actions as being energy, what kind of energy are we expressing? Aren't we responsible for the energy we express? We are either uplifting others with our positive energy, or we're adding more negativity to the world. We are either co-creating or co-destructing in each moment, and all of our moments count.

Awareness of what we are expressing in each moment is being conscious. Just knowing what we are expressing is not enough. The ultimate goal is choosing what to express in each moment. Accepting negative behavior as just being "the way I am" is a cop-out. When our buttons are being pushed, that is the time to take a pause and acknowledge what we are feeling. Once we know how we feel, we can push past the habitual reaction and make a conscious choice to take an alternate action. Isn't that using our free will?

Turning Poison into Medicine

The car was running, and we were late. It was Thursday morning, a school day, when the doorbell rang. I opened the door, and it was our landlord. The words came out of his mouth. "I've got bad news. You have 30 days to move out. But if you sign this paper and let the new owners come and see the property, you can have 60 days." What? They've sold the house right out from under us! My daughter was standing next to me and began asking questions. "We have to move?" "What about our pets?" "I don't want to lose our pets." She began to cry.

I tried to make sense of it all. I told the landlord I couldn't talk about it right then. I couldn't believe he said this in front of her. I told him I'd call him later, around 10:30 am. He left, and my daughter was still crying. We were devastated. I was so angry that he had made her cry I called him on his cell phone. He was so cold to me I just hung up on him. I had no idea what I would have said to him anyway.

Now before I continue, let me give you a little history. I had known the landlord since he was 11, and I was very close with his family. Over the summer he had offered to sell us this house. We had been renting it for four years and had talked about buying it one day. He said he would do what he could for us to buy it, and wanted us to have it. We settled on a price that was under market value, since we had been living there and had bettered the property. We also, I thought, were like family. He said if we couldn't come up with the money now, he would give us five years to buy it. He even offered us his loan guy, but we felt that might be a conflict of interest.

Three months went by. My husband had been ready, but I was dragging my feet. Was it fear operating or intuition? After all, we weren't in a hurry. He said we had five years. I decided to walk through my fear and trust in the outcome. If we were to have this house, we would. We found a loan company, had the papers drawn up and secured the loan. We called the landlord. He said he couldn't talk and would have to call us back.

Months went by without a call. We heard he had gotten married to his on-and-off-again girlfriend. Then we got a call from him saying he couldn't sell us the house, but we could still live there for up to 10 years. He said he had to hold it in trust for his daughter. That story didn't sound right. My intuition said his girlfriend, now spouse, didn't want us to have the house, especially when they could sell it for more money and make a bigger profit.

The next time we heard from the landlord was that Thursday he came to the door to tell us we had to move. I took my daughter to school that morning after the confrontation. When the clock hit 10:30 am, I was still so angry. I needed more time to call him, so I started cleaning the house, and cried my eyes out for the next hour and a half. By noon I was more calm and ready to talk. I got him on the phone, only now he didn't want to talk. He told me that it was out of his hands, and he was sending his wife over to deal with us. Not her, she had always been so mean-spirited, making it very clear that she disliked us.

His wife came to the door just as we were hanging up. She said in a very nasty and cold tone, "I've called the sheriff, and you have 30 days to get out." Easter Sunday was our evacuation date. Sweet! "We have a daughter," I said, hoping for a little compassion. "Aw..." she said with none.

Just then, words that hadn't come out of my mouth in years came hurling out. "You fucking bitch, get off the property." I burst into tears again. This time I think I cried more out of what came out of me than what they were doing to us. In that moment I had a realization of what Jesus meant when he said, and I'm paraphrasing, "What goes into you cannot defile you, it is what comes out of you that can." It's not what others do to you, but it's our reactions to circumstances and others that cause us the most harm. Intense.

The fact was, we had to pack up and move within 30 days whether we wanted to or not. Was it unfair? Maybe. There are always two sides to a story. Was I angry? Absolutely. The rest of that day I saw how that anger was alive only in those moments when I was living in the reaction to the situation and focusing on what the landlord had done to us. The reacting brought the past and future into the present moment. I was being filled with resentment and fear thoughts like "We're being screwed," and "We're going to be on the street," and an assortment of negative scenarios that were driving me into a victim state of consciousness. And with that state of mind, the anger grew in power. Was I going to stay in this anger and let it have its way with me? Did I really want to kick and scream and fight to hold on to this house? Did I want to spend all my energy trying to get revenge?

This is where a relationship with an infinite source of unconditional love really helps. My nighttime meditation gave me the answer. I would make a conscious choice how to walk through this move. I would take this seemingly negative situation and choose to look for an unexpected benefit, a blessing in disguise. I would choose to see this as an opportunity to grow spiritually and deepen my levels of trust and faith. I would transmute my anger into a beneficial energy, turning poison into medicine.

That night I turned to my family and asked them what they wanted in a new living space. Our daughter said she wanted a blue and white house, with an upstairs and downstairs. She wanted a pool, and a neighborhood with lots of kids. My husband wanted to buy a house and be out from under someone else's whims. I wanted my own meditation area. All of us wanted to be able to keep our family together, which included three cats, one California desert tortoise, one hamster, two white doves, and several fish.

I called everyone we knew and told them we were looking for a new place to live, preferably a house, but we were open. So many friends and people we didn't even know began to help us. Three days later the first house we looked at was it. More space, just a little more money, lots of kids on the street, and we could keep our pets.

I got my own meditation area, and the front of the house was even blue with white trim. Living in the anger would have closed us to this opportunity. The anger was the poison not the circumstance.

Choose to live a life where conscious choices are alive and reactions don't run you.

Conscious Choices

Imagine yourself on a sailboat. The waves are crashing in on you, the current is pulling you, and the wind is trying to blow you in every direction. Do you let go of the tiller, throw up your hands, and allow your boat to be pushed and pulled around by the elements, taking you where they may? Or do you hold on to that tiller and direct your course to where you will have it go, no matter what the wind, waves, and currents are doing?

The wind, the waves, and the currents represent the world, the people, and the circumstances in our lives. We are the boat. The tiller represents our conscious choices. When we give up our conscious choices, we are pushed and pulled by the world. We are run by our reactions, and we become victims of our circumstances.

When we use our conscious choices, we are able to determine our course. We take responsibility for our actions, and we use our free will, in each moment, to make adjustments along the way.

We all have a lot of experience and time invested in fear, doubt, anger, resentment, selfishness, guilt, self-pity, impatience, shame, lethargy, and pain. We have created habits out of our continued use of these energies. Most of these habits have been developed not by a conscious choosing to express these energies, but have come as a result of a reaction to someone, or something, outside of ourselves. Our anger, fear, impatience, doubt, and so forth, are reactionary. Some of these energies explode out of us before we even know what we are expressing. Being on a spiritual path gives us an opportunity to look at our actions and reactions. If need be, we can then make a conscious choice to express an energy that is of our own choosing, past the reaction to what is coming at us. We can develop new relationships and create new conscious habits transmuting fear into faith, doubt into trust, anger into forgiveness, ignorance into wisdom, judgment into compassion, impatience into patience, sadness into joy, restlessness into peace, and conditional love into unconditional love.

Forgiveness

Forgiveness is a choice, not a reaction. When we don't forgive others, we are choosing not to forgive. This choice leaves us with resentments and negative feelings inside. When someone has wronged or hurt us, we are left with justifiable anger, and this anger might be the deadliest of all. It gives us a good reason to be angry and tells us we have a right to be. As time goes by this anger doesn't go away. It hides inside of us and grows silently until we see that person again, or even think of that person, and now a resentment is attached to that anger. This anger is a poison that does us more harm than the person who harmed us in the first place.

In the act of forgiveness there are many levels. And in the levels of our forgiving process, we are called upon to make many, mini surrenders along the way. Forgiveness doesn't mean you have to have a relationship with that person. It doesn't even mean you have to have them over for dinner. It does mean that inside of your heart and mind you are free. Free of the resentment, the anger, and all the negative emotions and thoughts having to do with the person who harmed you. You then become free to express unconditional love and compassion to that person, be it from a distance or not. What comes out of us is what makes us who we are, not what others do to us.

We have all witnessed stories of unbelievable forgiveness. I remember crying my eyes out one day watching an Oprah show about a college student who had been hit by a drunk driver and was burned from head to toe. Her story was riveting. She was disfigured for life, and still she found a way to forgive the man who was driving. Her ability to forgive made her the most beautiful girl I had ever seen. She and her mother both found it in their hearts to choose forgiveness.

There are many degrees of harm. There's harm we do to ourselves and harm done to us. And some harm is unimaginable. Yet the poison caused by holding on to our anger and resentment is the same no matter what degree of harm we experience.

Here is an everyday run-of-the-mill story. A man got jealous of the attention his girlfriend was giving another man at a party. After the party was over, they had an argument. Cruel words were said in the heat of the moment, and they parted in anger. The next day his girlfriend told her friend what had happened and what he had said. The friend was outraged and advised her to break up with him. The man and his girlfriend had been struggling with their relationship for some time, and this was just the last straw, so his girlfriend asked him to move out. Although they stayed apart, she was open to a friendship. She chose to forgive him and let the hurt and anger go.

The man tried to maintain a friendship, but he was hurt and upset. He still blamed her friend for their breakup, and as the months went by, his anger towards her friend, turned to resentment. He felt the woman owed him an apology and felt justified in his anger. "If she admits she's wrong and asks for forgiveness, I'll give it to her." He continued, "Even the Lord wants you to ask for forgiveness, and if you don't ask, he doesn't give it." I offered him an alternate viewpoint. "Didn't Jesus say, 'Father, forgive them, for they know not what they do?' Wasn't he saying: forgive others even when they harm us, even when they are unconscious of their actions?"

Look at how much power this man was giving to that woman over his feelings and over his life. He was not going to let his anger go. He was unwilling to forgive her unless she asked for it. In his mind she was wrong. Until she apologized, he was going to keep his anger and resentment. The thing is, holding on to his anger and resentment wasn't hurting her anywhere near as much as it was hurting him. It was eating away at him, multiplying and poisoning his body, mind, and spirit. He was the one losing.

Once you know how you feel and you experience that feeling, you have a choice to stay in that feeling or let it go. How many people know that they can do that? How many people know that they are choosing anger? Most people think that they are angry because of someone or something on the outside of themselves making them angry. Our first reaction can be anger, but past that first reaction, and once you've identified that you are angry, if you continue to feel angry, then you are choosing that anger.

Now, if you don't know how you feel, of course you have no ability to make a choice and change how you feel. This is where being conscious is so important. Conscious of what we think and what we do, conscious of what energy we express, conscious of what we feel and what we say, and conscious of when we are reacting to a situation.

I have found that when we begin to work with this way of thinking about choice, we make a great deal of progress in letting go of negative emotions. We can also have a tendency to choose to stay in the very thing we need to release. After a while, we begin to see how ridiculous choosing that which harms us is. The more we choose to let go, the better we feel. We have to want to be willing to use our power of choice.

But what happens when we find we are unwilling? In the moment of being unwilling, there is always a seed of willingness ready to be sown. This is also where we can work with that infinite source we are building a relationship with. We can tune into the peace, joy, unconditional love, and wisdom inside ourselves and say, "I am unwilling. Show me how to be willing." In the silence, your honesty and your humility is heard, and like magic, willingness becomes yours. This is the best partnership there is. It's amazing what happens when we see our part in a relationship and make choices, instead of being at the mercy of our reactions.

Making conscious choices is the greatest power there is.
What choices are you making?

Faith or Fear

We are either, expressing faith, and living right now in the moment, or we are expressing fear, and living in the past or future. When we live in the moment, we feel empowered. Not a power coming from finite ego, but a power generated from an infinite source within. When our thoughts are in the past or in the future, we feel powerless. We feel powerless to effect change in our lives. In the Bible it says we cannot serve two masters at the same time. What if that meant we couldn't be in fear and faith at the same time? What would you choose?

We all seem to suffer from a lack of faith and trust. When we tune in daily in meditation, our faith and trust builds, and we begin to feel secure in who we are. We begin to know we are being cared for, and unconditionally loved. With our attention on tuning into love, how can we not feel this love?

A Wake-up Call

An acquaintance of mine was diagnosed with cancer of the bladder. We were talking one day, and soon I recognized how negative his thinking was. He was living in a headspace crowded with a constant stream of negative thoughts. He was consumed with fear, fear of dying, fear of being punished in some way, fear of living in pain and suffering, fear of leaving his family, fear that he would never be well again, fear of having the wrong doctor, and so on. These fears were running his life. They were behind every decision he was making and infected every one of his relationships.

He was motivated by fear, which led to doubts, then to worry, then to anxiety and panic. This then created a no-hope thinking and feeling scenario that literally colored every moment of his life. He was defenseless against his constant fear and his ensuing negative thinking. He had built this unconscious habit, years before his diagnosis, and had been living the role of a fearful man. He was defenseless because he was unaware of his habit of fear. In his mind that was just the way he was. He was his thoughts and his emotions.

I suggested that maybe this was his wake-up call, a wake-up call to see his habitual pattern of fear. I suggested that he had co-created this scenario with an infinite source, to teach himself how to recognize his habit of fear in his thinking and his actions. Once he could see where his fear was playing out, he had a choice to express the fear or change it into faith. Expressing faith would lead him to trust, and then to a sense of peace and well-being.

I could see the wheels turning inside his head. This was definitely a new concept for him. Did he want to stay in the fear and continue a negative downward spiral of no hope, or was he willing to take charge of his thoughts and transmute his fears? Could he find faith that he was right where he was supposed to be, and begin to choose to heal and live in the trust and gratitude of his life? He had a choice, whether the doctors could cure the cancer or not. The quality of his inner environment was in his hands. Fear shuts us down to our own inner healing and to our own well-being.

What is my life calling me to learn?

Taking Our Power Back

We are being bombarded with constant reminders to seek an outside cure. With the commercial media selling us solutions like, "If you have a disease, injury, or problem, whether it's mental or physical, take this, or that pill." We give up all our power to a solution on the outside of ourselves, whether it's a doctor, a pill, or other people's advice, while at the same time we stop doing any of the work we can do to co-contribute in our own healing.

I am not saying not to go to a doctor or take a pill. I am saying we have an obligation to ourselves to learn how to co-contribute and do our part. We have amazing abilities and healing powers right within ourselves. We just have to be willing to tap into our power and actualize it. The more we actualize our power, the more we will stop giving up our power. Why not get pro-active with your own health? When did we stop asking ourselves, "What is my part and my responsibility in my own health and healing?" Could it be just another one of our unconscious habits? Somehow we've gotten lost and given our power away. It's time to take our power back.

Trusting My Intuition

Now that I had given up all drugs and alcohol, I was looking to be healthy. A friend of mine took me to a Chinese herbalist. I gave him a history of my lifestyle thus far, and he sent me for a blood test. The results were that I had a non-A, non-B hepatitis. This was in 1984, and there was no name for hepatitis C back then. He began to treat me with a very funky tea with all these strange-looking roots in it. The tea tasted horrible, but I managed to drink it faithfully for weeks, maybe months. Months later, he looked at my blood again and said I was better.

Ten years later I had another blood test at the request of a new doctor I was seeing. He said I had hepatitis C and wanted me to see a liver specialist. So I went to see a liver specialist, and he started filling my head with all this doom and gloom about what hepatitis C can do to you, and how it could turn into cancer of the liver and all this fear-based information. He said I needed to go on interferon, a drug designed to cure hepatitis C. I said I really didn't think I needed the drug. I had been treated with Chinese medicine years ago for this, and I was all right. He wanted to do a liver biopsy anyway, and he said if the hepatitis C was minimal, I wouldn't need the interferon.

If I wasn't as strong-minded as I am, I would have gotten sicker that day. He was selling me the disease to sell me the cure. At another time in my life, I would have bought that fear and internalized it and made it real. In that moment I saw how so many of us have no defense over fear-based information. We internalize it and make it real, without even knowing we're doing it.

I agreed to the biopsy. Not for myself. I did it for my mom who was worried about me. She was buying that fear package, and I did it to ease her mind. The result of the biopsy was minimal, just as I thought. He still tried to sell me the cure, even after he had said I wouldn't need the interferon if the results were minimal. The interferon just did not feel right to me.

I decided to tap into my own power and inner healing. I began to work with a visualization technique to see and create a healthy liver. I also had a friend who was an acupuncturist and herbalist. He gave me acupuncture and more funky Chinese tea.

Seven years later another doctor asked for another blood test. He then suggested a second liver biopsy. This specialist would be able to compare two slices of my liver and see what had or had not occurred in seven years. I agreed and told him the story I've just told you. When we got the results back, he said that the inflammation had lessened and that I was right: the damage was minimal, and I'd probably die from something else. There was a change. My liver was better.

I sought out alternative ways to heal because the Western way in this instance didn't feel right to me. I listened to my intuition and followed it. I chose to co-contribute in my own inner healing by practicing positive affirmations and this healing technique:

Give the illness or injury a color and a texture. Let's say red and rough. Then visualize that color and texture changing into, let's say, blue and smooth for perfect health and all-healed.

See in your mind's eye the red changing into blue, the rough changing into the smooth. Repeat this visualization morning and night and anytime you think of the injury or illness throughout the day.

Beyond the Obvious

A healing technique is something you can do actively to be part of the healing process. You can use it right along with a doctor when you need a doctor's help. Why allow your mind to revolve negative thoughts of doubt, motivated by fear-based thinking, in your consciousness? Thoughts such as, "I am not going to heal. I'm going to die. This is going to take forever. I'm never going to get better. I am in pain," et cetera, are all negative thoughts motivated by fear. If you are motivated by fear, you negate any ability of your own self-healing. You force yourself to seek only an outside answer and give all your power away.

I was at my daughter's gymnastics class one afternoon, and a young teenage girl came hobbling off the mats crying, and in pain. Her father and others gathered around her saying, "Where does it hurt? Are you all right? Do you need an Advil? You probably need to go to the hospital. Put some ice on it." All of their comments were about getting outside help, and their voices had a tone of dread and worry. All she could do was continue to cry. I was sitting next to her and wanted to help. I began to tell her how amazing the human body was and how it was already beginning to heal itself. I told her that she had power within herself to assist the healing by using her mind, her thoughts, and by visualizing her recovery. Then I gave her the healing technique I used on my liver. As I spoke she calmed down. She heard me. I asked her if she understood what I was saying and she did.

Ten minutes later, her father and she were talking about why this happened. She was telling him what she'd been doing right before the injury. I leaned over again and suggested that perhaps it had nothing to do with gymnastics at all. Perhaps it took place to teach her at this moment in her life about her own abilities, power, and self-healing. And perhaps it happened to teach her the part she can play in her own health.

There is always something deeper going on in our lives if we look for it. There is always a lesson we can learn if we choose to look beyond the obvious.

Great out of the Gate

I was born in June just after one in the morning Eastern Standard Time. My mother said I was an easy birth, only one and a half hours from first labor pain. I whooshed out into the world with a readiness and a confidence, followed by 20 hours a day of screaming and crying for the next six months. My mother thought it was her milk, so she stopped nursing me after two months. She tried everything to comfort and care for me, but nothing worked.

I can just see myself in the Astral getting ready to come back to earth again. Knowing just what I had to accomplish, I was ready, willing, and confident, until I got here, then, "WAIT!" screaming in a panic. "I made a mistake. I'm not ready." "I didn't read the fine print! Listen, there's got to be an easier way." I'm not ready to overcome my self-centeredness or any other major defect of character." "Wait, I was just kidding!"

This behavior followed me for years, great out of the gate, and then crying and screaming, and digging my heels in. The moment I arrived, I realized just what I had gotten myself into, yet again.

When my mother took me to the doctor to find out what was wrong with me, he called it "colic."

Little did he know I was just balking at another tour.

Image by R. F. Leigh

Soul Evolution

A thought came to me in meditation the other night about our soul's evolution and the journey it takes through incarnations. Charles Darwin's Theory of Evolution is about our physical transformation throughout the ages. What about the evolution of our consciousness, and our own soul's evolution?

It seems to me what makes us different is our consciousness, not the color of our skin or our language or our religion. We all have different degrees of consciousness here on earth. When we meditate, we elevate our consciousness and begin to see our similarities and our differences disappear. Our consciousness expands and evolves as we grow spiritually. Prejudice and ignorance fade, and we begin to experience a connection to all life.

My Journey with Paramahansa Yogananda

He clearly knew me before I knew him. When I first saw his picture in the windmill chapel I wrote in my journal, "He reminds me of me." I recognized the joy that was shining out of his face. At that time I wasn't aware he was the author of *Metaphysical Meditations*, and when I look back on the sequence of events leading up to today, I can see how he was silently guiding me and calling me back home.

Probably the first time I ever saw Paramahansa Yogananda's picture was in 1985 at the house of a classmate while rehearsing an acting scene. He had his picture hanging on the wall, but I don't remember talking with him about Yogananda. The next time was in 1988 at the Bodhi Tree bookstore, where I had bought his book to use in my mirror work. At that time I still hadn't put any of this together. I also still wasn't aware of who he was. I was just attracted to his words.

1989 was the first year I was taken to the Lake Shrine in Pacific Palisades at the Self-Realization Fellowship. That was when I looked at his picture on the wall in the windmill chapel, and saw a part of myself in his eyes. At that time

I began reading the *Autobiography of a Yogi*, his life story, and his words brought tears to my eyes. I related so deeply. I went to a few services at the Lake Shrine, but I didn't hear about the lessons you could take. I obviously wasn't ready. I got into another "desert" relationship right in the middle of reading his autobiography. I had to be out in the world for two more years without him while he waited patiently for me.

I had now been meditating 20 minutes once a day for three years. Near the end of that two-year "desert" relationship, I heard inside of myself in meditation one morning that my meditation was going to change. It was not a voice like Charlton Heston heard in the movie *The Ten Commandments*. It was more like silent information. My first response was fear, fear of the unknown and fear of change. I was comfortable with the meditation I was doing. It took me three days of wrestling with the fear to reach a surrendered state. I was ready to move forward. That morning, three days later, at the end of my meditation, I got on my knees and simply said, "Show me where I'm going." "I am willing."

That evening I went out to dinner with my soon-to-be ex-boyfriend and a friend of his from New York. Unbelievably, his friend was in town attending the Self-Realization Fellowship's

Convocation, held in downtown Los Angeles every year for a week. It was like a light bulb going off inside of me. I knew now what the silent information meant. I knew how my meditation was going to change. Yogananda was speaking to me, and I heard him. When the student is ready, the teacher appears. And I was ready.

The next morning I was on the phone to the S.R.F. Mother Center to send away for his life lessons. In the lessons I would receive new techniques of meditation, and after studying for a year, I would get a scientific form of meditation to practice called Kriya Yoga. I had started meditating in 1988, but it wasn't until that day in 1991, when I got on my knees and became willing for my meditation to change, that the door opened, and there he was. Yogananda had always been there waiting for me to wake up and remember who I was and where I was going. Come on little girl, was his gentle whispering in my heart. I could hear it now.

I am still meditating and practicing Kriya Yoga twice a day. I tell you of my journey with Yogananda, not to sell you this path, but to share with you where my first years of meditation led me. There are many spiritual paths and many forms of meditation. And I don't know if you will ever choose a specific path or even where meditation will lead you. But I do know, that if you begin to meditate on a daily basis, the magnitude of joy, unconditional love, wisdom, and peace you will uncover within yourself will fulfill you like nothing else.

I will give you the meditation I started with. Use it as a starting point. See where it leads you. Your consciousness and your life will transform in ways that will amaze you.

"When you will have expanded that consciousness by meditation and thinking of others, you will no longer be a limited human being, identified with the selfish ego-centered perspective of your one body. You will feel your greater Self in everyone."

-Paramahansa Yogananda

A Meditation in 5 Parts

Here is the meditation I practiced for the first 3 ½ years. This will give you a way to begin if you haven't found your way already.

Sit up straight with legs crossed and your palms turned upward and open. If sitting cross-legged is painful, or brings with it a body consciousness, sit in a chair keeping your spine away from the back of the chair, and your feet solidly planted on the ground. You want to feel an elongation of your spine while keeping your shoulders back. Most importantly, have a relaxation about this. The point between your eyebrows is where you will place your gaze. This is called the spiritual eye. You can do this by looking up to that point and then gently closing your eyes, again with a relaxation as opposed to a straining.

1. Begin with a prayer inwardly or out loud. A wonderful way to pray is to speak from the language of your heart. There is no wrong way to pray when we are sincere.

2. Breathe in through your nose to a count of ten. Hold that breath for ten counts. Then release your breath through your mouth for a count of ten. Repeat this several times.

Then allow your breath to flow freely in and out as it may. Be an observer of your breath.

3. In your mind silently repeat a short spiritual thought called a mantra. Such as "I am peace," "I am spirit," "Peace like a river flows through me," or "I am the active expression of unconditional love at all times." That was my first mantra. Come up with a mantra that touches you, that means something to you. The mantra enables your restless mind to have a one-pointed spiritual focus. As you begin to repeat your mantra, your mind may begin to wander into past thoughts and then into future thoughts. As soon as you notice this happening, just begin your mantra again. Always keep coming back to your spiritual thought.

4. Once you have calmed your mind and drawn your outward flowing energy inward, you may begin to feel a stillness and a silence. There may be a sense of peace or joy. Sit here for a while. Remember your experiences may vary from day to day. Whatever you experience, it is perfect for you right as it's happening. Some days your head may be consumed with one thought after another. Another day you might be weeping with tears of gratitude, feeling connected to all

living things. If you do experience joy, or peace, or unconditional love, or wisdom inside of you and around you, tune into these energies, feel the connection, and allow for a deepening and a oneness with these energies. You are that joy, peace, wisdom, and unconditional love.

5. Nearing the end of your meditation let the fountain of your love pour out in gratitude for all that you have, and all that you don't have. Less passionately, say what you're grateful for. There is always something to be grateful for. One day you will feel the perfectness of you, a connection to all life, and a gratitude that will pour out of your heart for everyone and everything in your life. Showing up and making the effort to meditate on a daily basis is all you need to do.

You can also begin a meditation with a visualization.

A Visualization

With eyes closed, visualize in your mind a rough sea at night. See the waves crashing into each other, one after the other. Picture this very tumultuous sea. See the full moon shining. Notice its reflection is unclear, as it highlights the foam of the crashing waves. Now see the waves begin to dissolve slowly one by one. With each breath you take, see the waves slowly subside. The sea is completely still now, with no ripples at all. Look at the full moon. See the moon's reflection crystal clear in the water. Now imagine that you are the sea and the moon is unconditional love, peace, joy, and wisdom. Sit here for a while. Only in the stillness can the full moon truly be reflected.

The crashing waves are our thoughts. When we still our thoughts, we can more easily connect to the full moon of joy, peace, unconditional love and wisdom in meditation. We then can more easily reflect these energies out into our world.

Remember, I began with a realistic goal of five minutes a day, and little by little, I increased to 20 minutes a day. I did this for three and a half years until my meditation led me to a specific spiritual path. I then went from once to twice a day, with a minimum of 30 minutes each time. Before my daughter was born I was meditating one hour and fifteen minutes morning and night, and Friday nights going to a three-hour meditation. I have been meditating now for 21 years, and practicing Kriya Yoga for the last 17.

I couldn't possibly describe what has transpired in every meditation I've had until now. But I can say I have had my struggles. I have pushed through many restless moments, cried in pain and in joy. I have felt connected and not connected, but no matter what, I have made a daily effort. I tell you this to inspire you, not to overwhelm you. Meditation has transformed my inner and outer world more than anything else I have ever done. I know if you begin to meditate daily, you will be guided from within to your highest consciousness and to your best you in this lifetime. You can take this anywhere you want it to go.

Forever Grateful

Writing this book is my way of giving back all the understandings, truths, and tools I have discovered along this great and continuing spiritual journey. Even in my darkest moments, there has always been a greater purpose at work.

My sincerest desire is that this book inspires you to find your own "Silent M.a.g.i.c." and to use these remedies to transform your life. May I inspire in you a reason to get off the roller coaster of emotional ups and downs, and to find your own inner happiness, joy, and personal power. May I inspire in you a reason to question, discover, and cultivate a personal relationship with an infinite source that you can tune into and co-create with in your life. And may I inspire in you a reason to build a deeper, more loving relationship with yourself and others by using these tools to retrain and replace negative habitual thinking and actions with positive thoughts and conscious choices.

I am forever grateful to my past for bringing me to this glorious present. May you find your own gratitude for each and every moment of your life.

Silent M.a.g.i.c.

M .... Meditation

A .... Affirmations

G .... Gratitude

I .... Inward motivation

C .... Conscious choices

and Other Remedies

Use a Loving Microscope

Be a Co-Creator

See Opportunities in the Face of Obstacles

Look Beyond the Obvious

Be Willing to Let Go

Find Forgiveness in Your Heart

Ask what your Life is Calling you to Learn

www.ingramcontent.com/pod-product-compliance
Ingram Content Group UK Ltd.
Pitfield, Milton Keynes, MK11 3LW, UK
UKHW041958230426
12048UKWH00008B/406